Ball of Light

Balboa Press books may be ordered through booksellers or by contacting:

Balboa Press
A Division of Hay House
1663 Liberty Drive
Bloomington, IN 47403
www.balboapress.com
1 (877) 407-4847

Interior Image Credit: Christina McAfoos

ISBN: 978-1-9822-4667-9 (sc)
978-1-9822-4668-6 (e)

Library of Congress Control Number: 2020907082

Print information available on the last page.

Balboa Press rev. date: 05/07/2020

BALBOA.PRESS
A DIVISION OF HAY HOUSE

Ball of Light

Christina McAfoos

Dedicated to my supportive husband
Mike and our beautiful children.

I am a girl.
I am a ball of light.

I have a friend.

He is a ball of light too.

There is a big ball of light above my head. I am connected to it. We are connected by a tube of light.

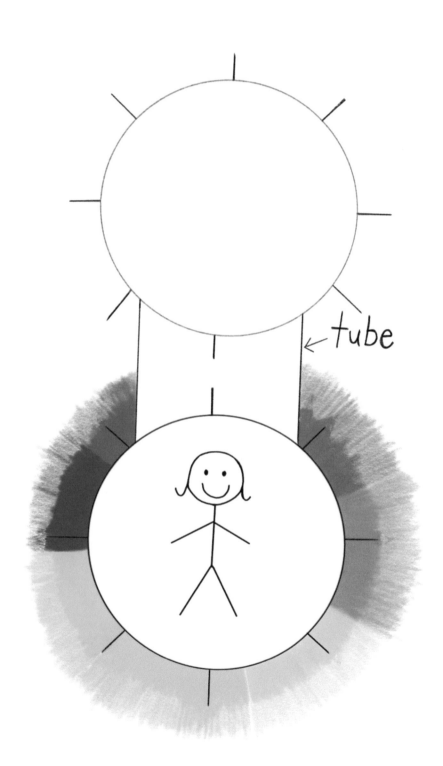

tube

I can make my ball of light bigger or smaller by letting the light out, or keeping it in.

My light expands when I allow it to flow out. The more light I let out, the more light comes down.

My ball of light becomes smaller because I block the light from coming out. The big ball of light notices that it doesn't need to send any more light down the tube.

less light needed this way

My ball of light is my aura. My light grows bigger when I allow it to shine. My aura glows brighter when I let more light out. I love my light.

It feels much better when the light flows out. The flow of light going out makes me feel energized and happy.

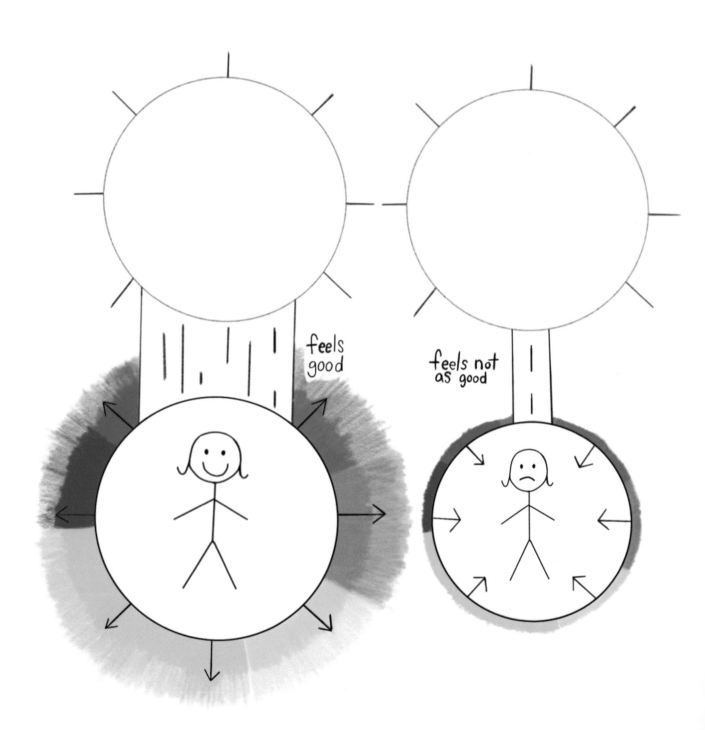

You are a ball of light too.

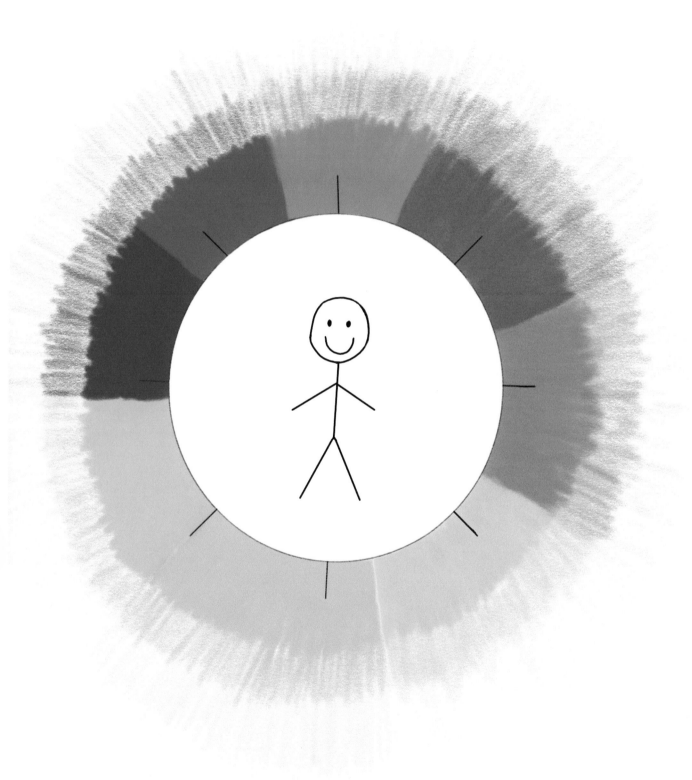

Our lights touch each other even if we can't see it.

When we share our light,
our light gets bigger.

Some don't share their light.

Sharing our light makes other people feel better.

When we share our light, others feel it.

We always have an endless supply of light that comes down from the big ball of light. We can't see the big ball of light because of a circle in the middle of our tube. Some call it a veil.

← circle

The light flows down, and our circle spins. The more light that comes down the faster the circle spins. It feels good when it spins fast.

spins

When we don't let the light flow, our circle spins slow, so it gets off balance. It wobbles. This doesn't feel good.

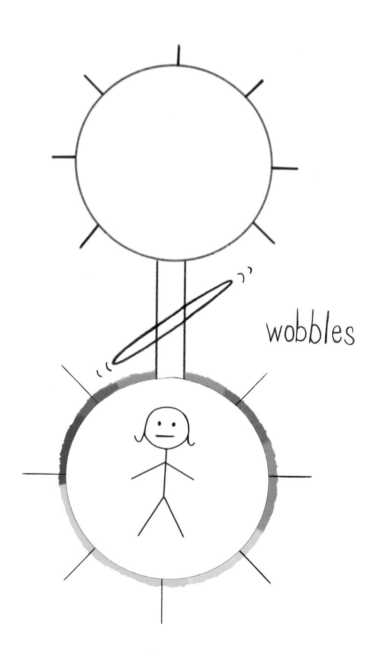

wobbles

When I'm happy, it's like
sparkles of light rain down.

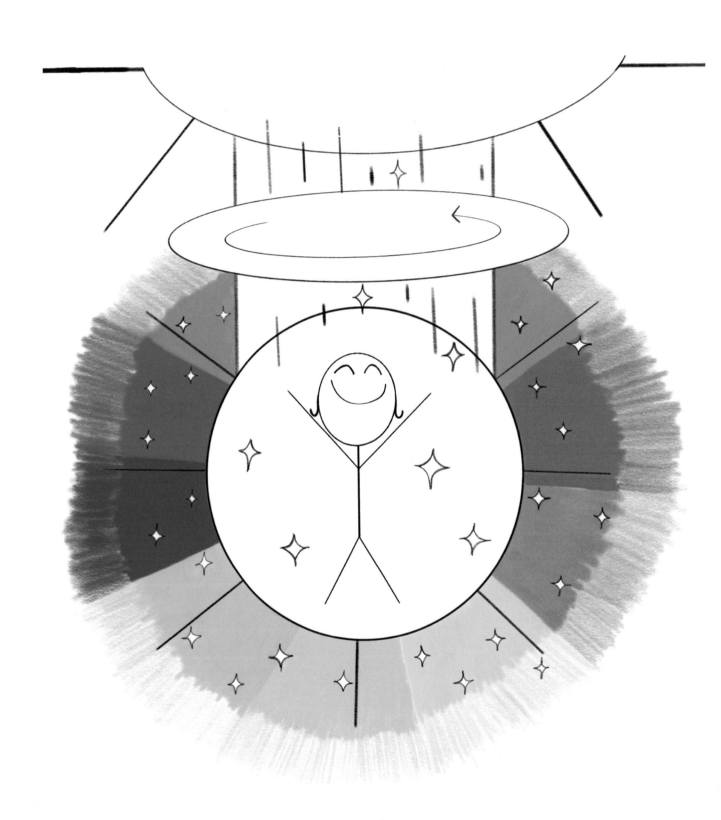

Sometimes my light feels faded, and I don't understand why. When I'm sad, it feels like the sparkles stopped. My feelings affect my ball of light.

Anytime I feel fear, I can choose to think happy thoughts on purpose. It's amazing how well this works.

I can recharge my ball of light
by resting or connecting to
my source of light within.

I can make my ball of light grow
bigger when I am grateful.

I can also make my ball of light bigger
and more sparkly by being kind to others.

My light gets bigger when I do things that make me happy.

My ball of light, my aura, radiates out like waves of energy. The light goes out in a vibration. The light vibrates at different colors, different frequencies.

Our balls of light are different colors.
People are like pretty rainbows.

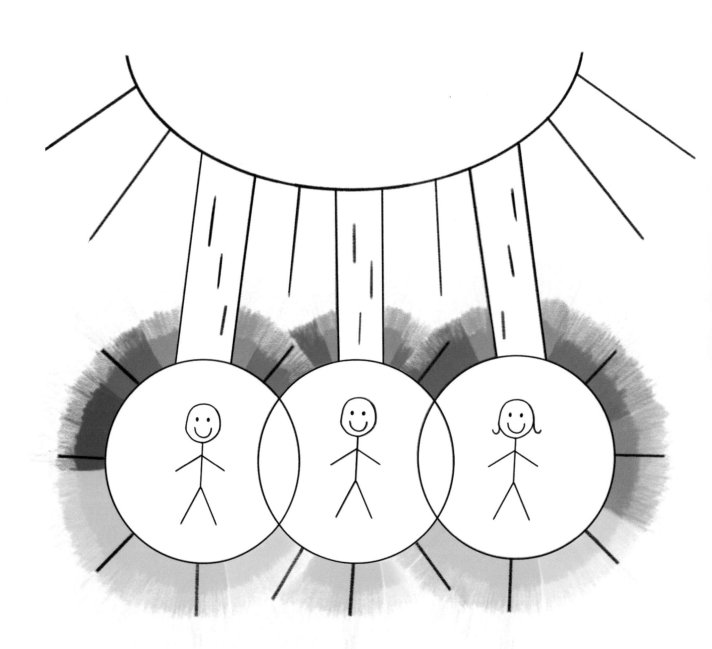

The big ball of light is a rainbow too.

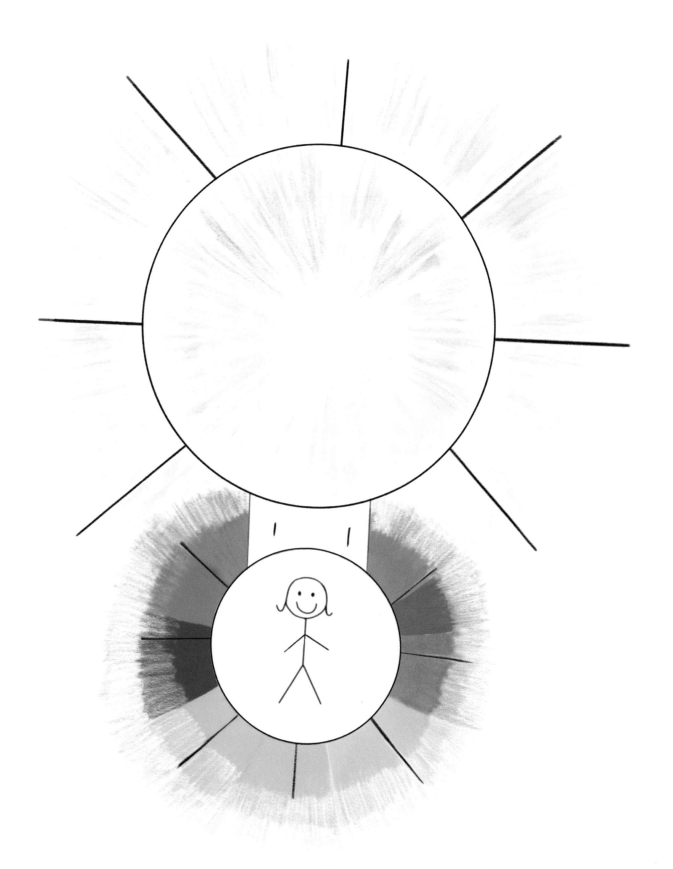

I am the big ball of light. We all are. We are one big ball of light. The universe is a big ball of light. I am it. It is me. We are one. One light.

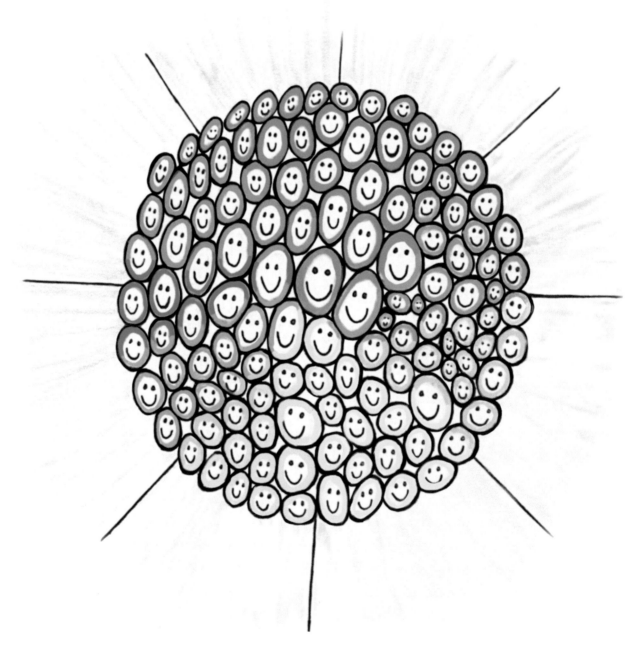

One ball of light.

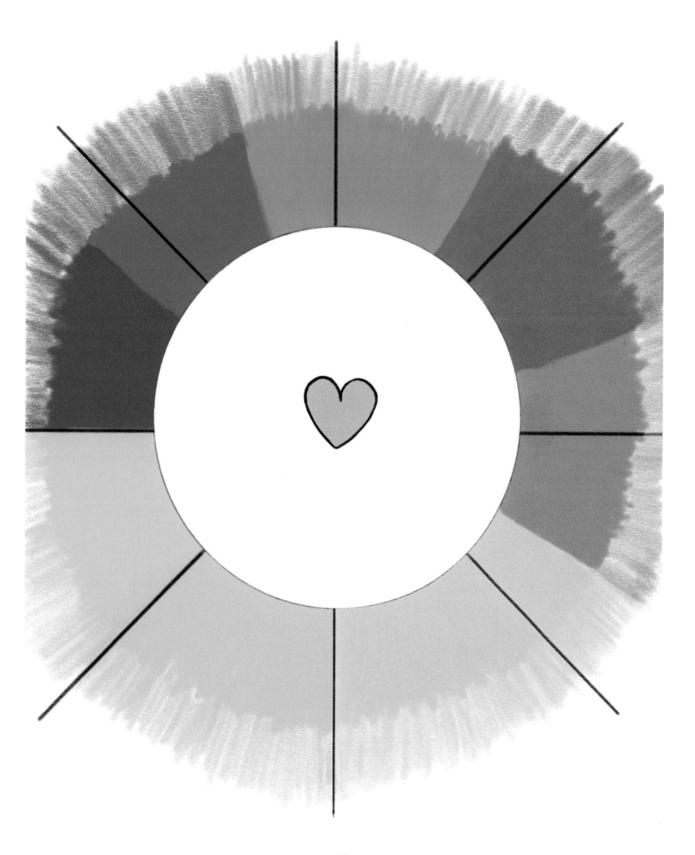

Printed in the United States
By Bookmasters